PORTLAND DIVE BARS PASSPORT

Volume 2

KC Shomler

Steven Shomler

Arthur Breur

Bonfire Books Press

Bonfire

BOOKS

Press

Contents

Introduction

We had such a blast doing Volume 1 of the Portland Dive Bar Passport, we couldn't resist doing another.

So here it is!

Another four routes comprised of 16 dives, lovingly curated for your dive bar touring pleasure.

We are profoundly lucky to live in Portland, where dive bars are celebrated, abundant and quirky as hell.

Go! Have fun!

And remember: be a good patron, tip well, be kind. Dive bars and their inhabitants deserve the utmost respect.

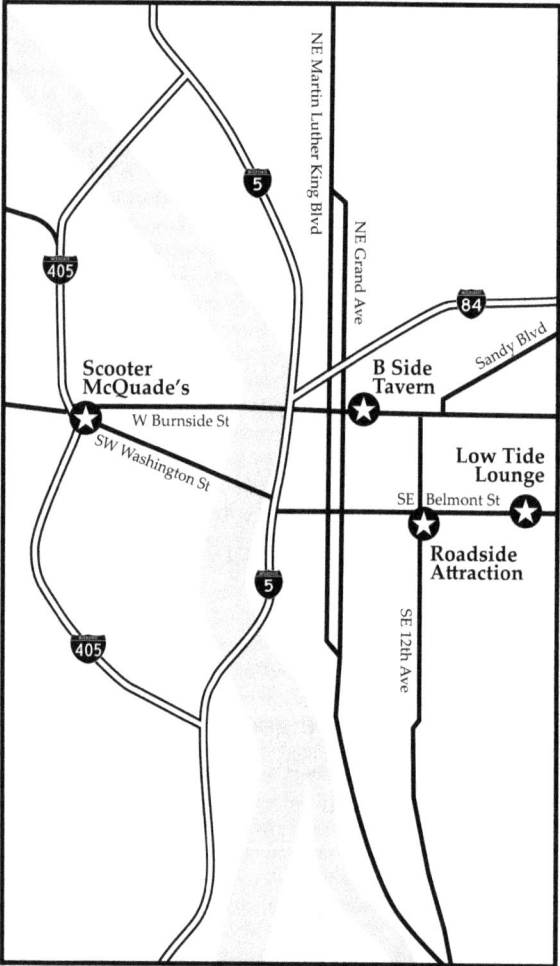

NE Martin Luther King Blvd

NE Grand Ave

84

Sandy Blvd

5

405

Scooter McQuade's

W Burnside St

SW Washington St

B Side Tavern

Low Tide Lounge

SE Belmont St

SE 12th Ave

Roadside Attraction

5

405

Route 1

Scooter McQuade's
B Side Tavern
Roadside Attraction
Low Tide Lounge

Scooter McQuade's

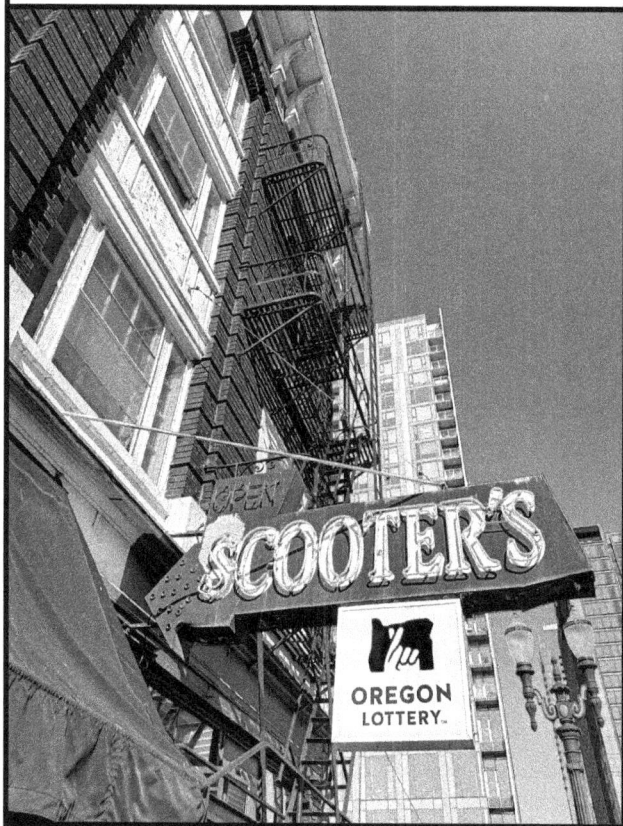

ADDRESS: 1321 SW Washington St

OUR THOUGHTS

WHY WE THINK YOU SHOULD VISIT:
Great food, great music, great service, great spot.

GOOD FOR EATING OR JUST DRINKING?
Both.

YOUR TURN

DATES VISITED: _____

WORTHY OF A RETURN VISIT? _____

IMPRESSIONS: _____

_____

_____

_____

_____

_____

B Side Tavern

Address: 632 E Burnside St

OUR THOUGHTS

WHY WE THINK YOU SHOULD VISIT:
Top-notch bathroom graffiti.

GOOD FOR EATING OR JUST DRINKING?
Just drinking.

YOUR TURN

DATES VISITED: _____

WORTHY OF A RETURN VISIT? _____

IMPRESSIONS: _____

_____

_____

_____

_____

_____

_____

Roadside Attraction

A ROADSIDE ATTRACTION 1000 S.E. 12th

ADDRESS: 1000 SE 12th Ave

OUR THOUGHTS

WHY WE THINK YOU SHOULD VISIT:
A world of wonderful oddities in a wacky, mostly outdoor, but sheltered setting.

GOOD FOR EATING OR JUST DRINKING?
Both. Fancy food, so bring a wad of bills since it is cash only.

YOUR TURN

DATES VISITED: _____

WORTHY OF A RETURN VISIT? _____

IMPRESSIONS: _____

_____

_____

_____

_____

_____

_____

Low Tide Lounge

ADDRESS: 2045 SE Belmont St

OUR THOUGHTS

WHY WE THINK YOU SHOULD VISIT:
Low-tech heaven with a pleasing lack of machines except a free-play jukebox.

GOOD FOR EATING OR JUST DRINKING?
Both (good vegan/veg spot).

YOUR TURN

DATES VISITED: _____

WORTHY OF A RETURN VISIT? _____

IMPRESSIONS: _____

_____

_____

_____

_____

_____

_____

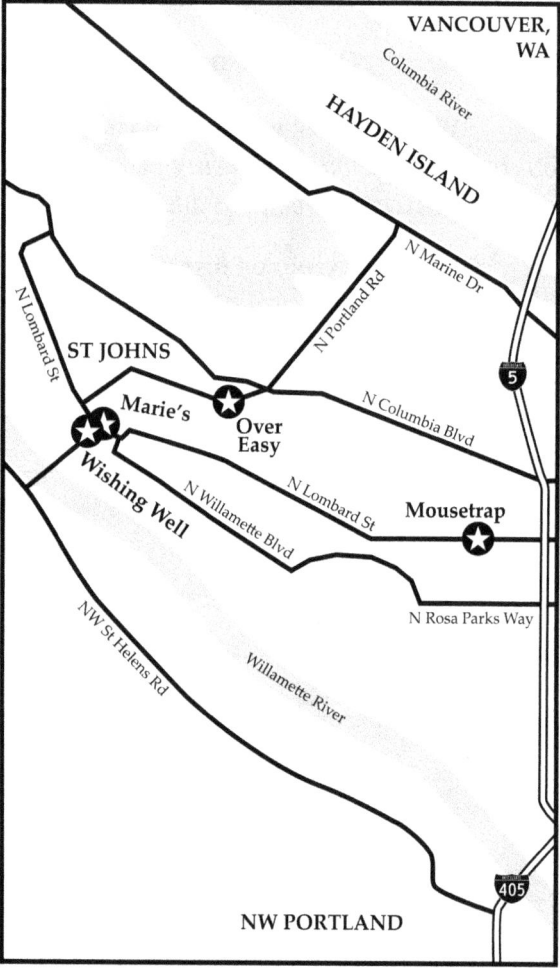

VANCOUVER, WA

Columbia River

HAYDEN ISLAND

N Marine Dr

N Lombard St

ST JOHNS

N Portland Rd

N Columbia Blvd

I-5

Marie's

Over Easy

Wishing Well

N Willamette Blvd

N Lombard St

Mousetrap

NW St Helens Rd

N Rosa Parks Way

Willamette River

NW PORTLAND

405

Route 2

Mousetrap Tavern
Over Easy Bar
Marie's
Wishing Well

Mousetrap Tavern

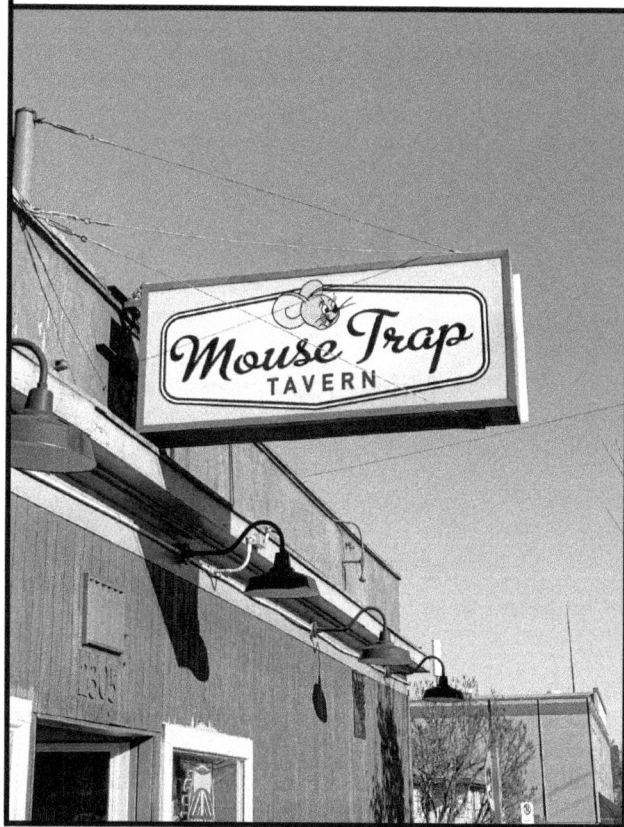

Address: 2305 N Lombard St

Our Thoughts

Why we think you should visit:
Solid neighborhood joint. Extensive fried foods menu, if that's your thing.

Good for eating or just drinking?
Both (if you're not concerned about your cholesterol).

Your Turn

Dates Visited: _____

Worthy of a return visit? _____

Impressions: _____

_____

_____

_____

_____

_____

Over Easy Bar

ADDRESS: 6801 N Columbia Way

OUR THOUGHTS

WHY WE THINK YOU SHOULD VISIT:
The TV star of dive bars (featured on season 4 of Dive Bar Rescue under its previous moniker of the 6-Point Inn).

GOOD FOR EATING OR JUST DRINKING?
Both.

YOUR TURN

DATES VISITED: _____

WORTHY OF A RETURN VISIT? _____

IMPRESSIONS: _____

_____

_____

_____

_____

_____

Marie's

Address: 8727 N Lombard St

Our Thoughts

Why we think you should visit:
The secret garden out back.

Good for eating or just drinking?
Just drinking.

Your Turn

Dates Visited: _____

Worthy of a return visit? _____

Impressions: _____

_____

_____

_____

_____

_____

_____

Wishing Well

ADDRESS: 8800 N Lombard St

OUR THOUGHTS

WHY WE THINK YOU SHOULD VISIT:
Cheap and good Chinese food, stiff drinks.

GOOD FOR EATING OR JUST DRINKING?
Both.

YOUR TURN

DATES VISITED: _____

WORTHY OF A RETURN VISIT? _____

IMPRESSIONS: _____

_____

_____

_____

_____

_____

Route 3

Bar of the Gods
Dots Café
Cosmo Lounge
Misdemeanor Meadows

Bar of the Gods

ADDRESS: 4801 SE Hawthorne Blvd

OUR THOUGHTS

WHY WE THINK YOU SHOULD VISIT:
Great rock 'n' roll vibe and late night eats.

GOOD FOR EATING OR JUST DRINKING?
Both.

YOUR TURN

DATES VISITED: _____

WORTHY OF A RETURN VISIT? _____

IMPRESSIONS: _____

_____

_____

_____

_____

_____

_____

Dots Café

ADDRESS: 2521 SE Clinton St

OUR THOUGHTS

WHY WE THINK YOU SHOULD VISIT:
*Fabulous velvet paintings, flocked wallpaper,
and lots of tasty vegan options on the menu.*

GOOD FOR EATING OR JUST DRINKING?
Both.

YOUR TURN

DATES VISITED: _____

WORTHY OF A RETURN VISIT? _____

IMPRESSIONS: _____

_____

_____

_____

_____

_____

_____

Cosmo Lounge

Address: 6707 SE Milwaukie Ave

OUR THOUGHTS

WHY WE THINK YOU SHOULD VISIT:
Quintessential dive bar: a small hole in the wall ideally designed for a quick, stiff drink.

GOOD FOR EATING OR JUST DRINKING?
Just drinking.

YOUR TURN

DATES VISITED: _____

WORTHY OF A RETURN VISIT? _____

IMPRESSIONS: _____

_____

_____

_____

_____

_____

Misdemeanor Meadows

ADDRESS: 6920 SE 52nd Ave

OUR THOUGHTS

WHY WE THINK YOU SHOULD VISIT:
Late night spot known for live music. Excellent eclectic vibe.

GOOD FOR EATING OR JUST DRINKING?
Just drinking.

YOUR TURN

DATES VISITED: _____

WORTHY OF A RETURN VISIT? _____

IMPRESSIONS: _____

_____

_____

_____

_____

_____

_____

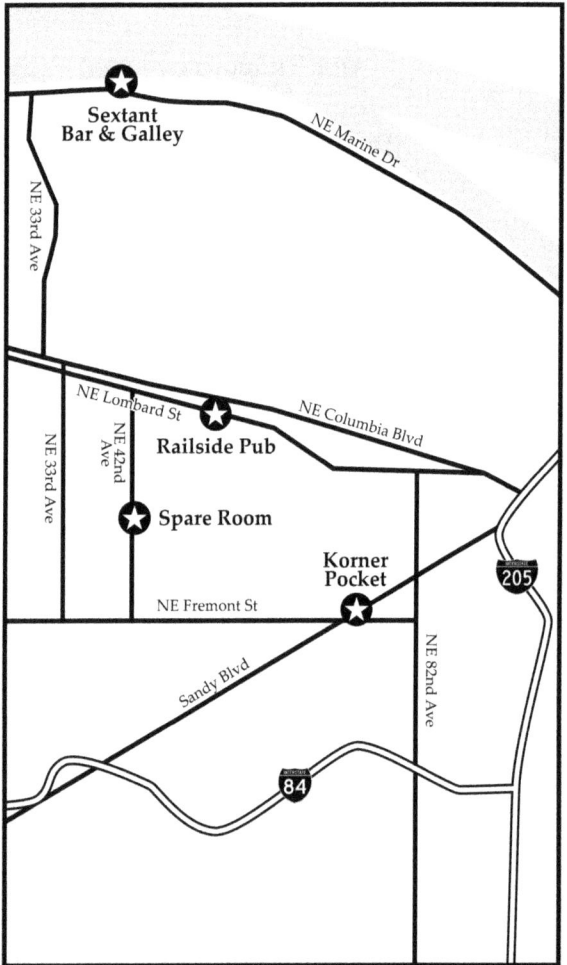

Route 4

Sextant Bar & Galley
Railside Pub
Spare Room
Korner Pocket

Sextant Bar & Galley

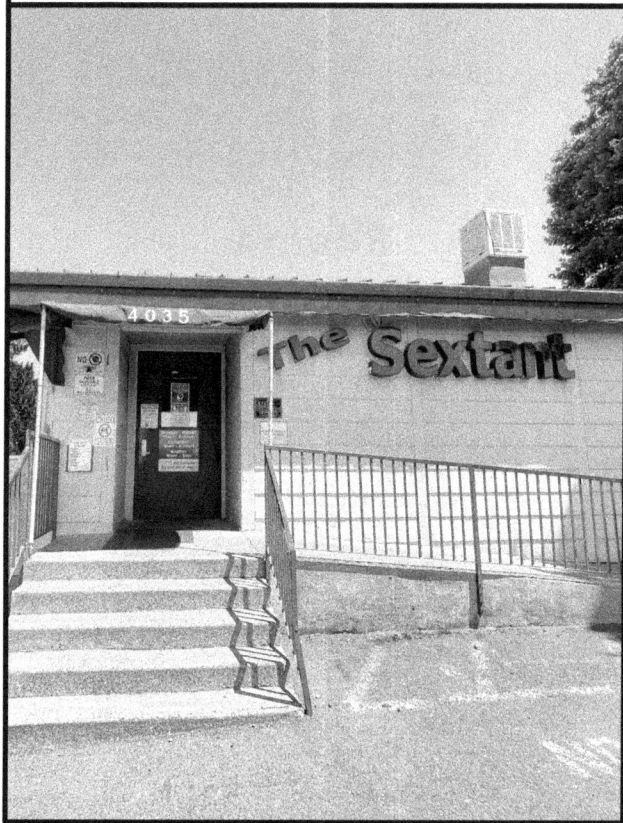

Address: 4035 NE Marine Dr

Our Thoughts

Why we think you should visit:
Dive bar with a river view? Yes indeed!

Good for eating or just drinking?
Both.

Your Turn

Dates Visited: _____

Worthy of a return visit? _____

Impressions: _____

_____

_____

_____

_____

_____

Railside Pub

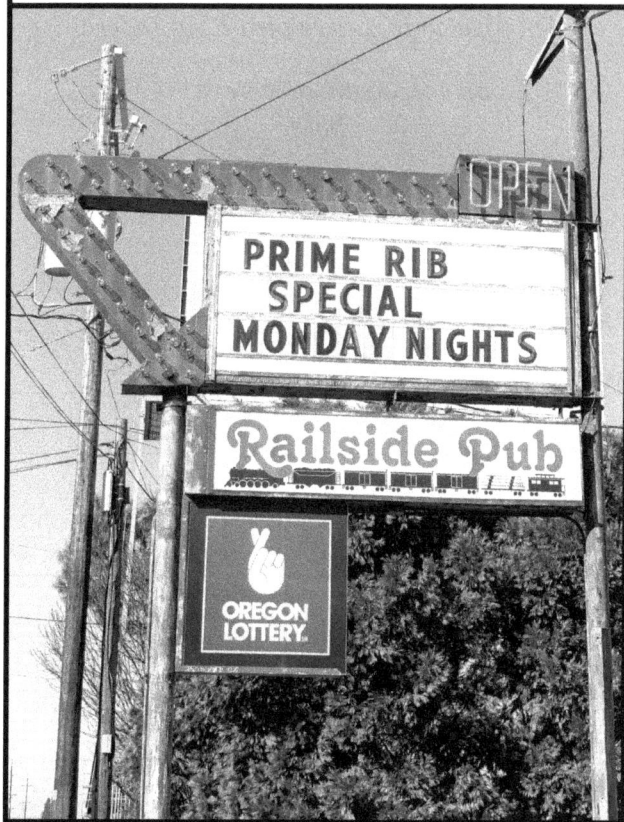

Address: 5301 NE Portland Hwy

Our Thoughts

Why we think you should visit:
Great quality food, large portions.

Good for eating or just drinking?
Both.

Your Turn

Dates Visited: _____

Worthy of a return visit? _____

Impressions: _____

_____

_____

_____

_____

_____

_____

Spare Room

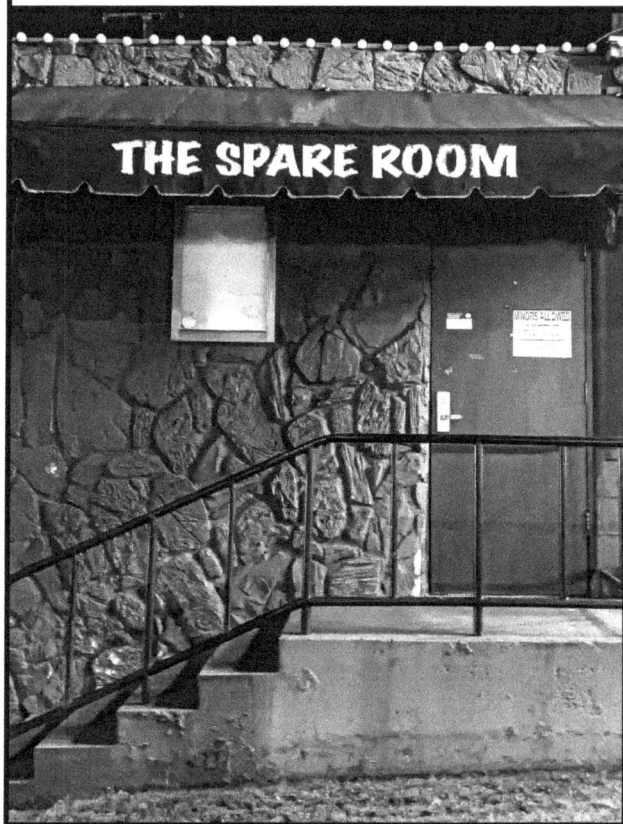

ADDRESS: 4830 NE 42nd Ave

OUR THOUGHTS

WHY WE THINK YOU SHOULD VISIT:
*Drink specials, breakfast served all day,
damn good bacon.*

GOOD FOR EATING OR JUST DRINKING?
Both.

YOUR TURN

DATES VISITED: _____

WORTHY OF A RETURN VISIT? _____

IMPRESSIONS: _____

_____

_____

_____

_____

_____

_____

Korner Pocket

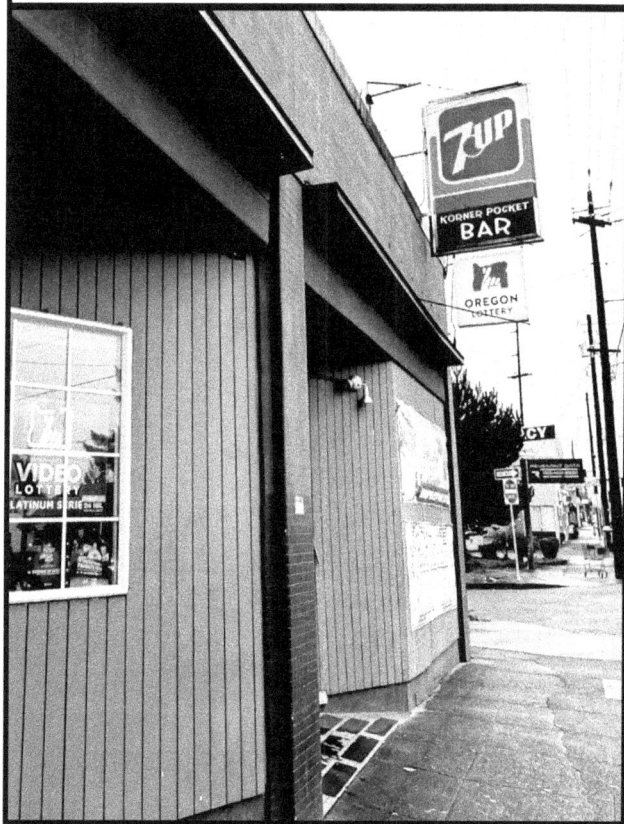

Address: 7300 NE Sandy Blvd

Our Thoughts

Why we think you should visit:
Open early. Homey, well-tended spot.

Good for eating or just drinking?
*Just drinking, although they do have
fried delights and hot dogs.*

Your Turn

Dates Visited: _____

Worthy of a return visit? _____

Impressions: _____

_____

_____

_____

_____

_____

CHECKLIST

Route 1 ☐
   Scooter McQuade's ☐
   B Side Tavern ☐
   Roadside Attraction ☐
   Low Tide Lounge ☐

Route 2 ☐
   Mousetrap Tavern ☐
   Over Easy Bar ☐
   Marie's ☐
   Wishing Well ☐

Route 3 ☐
   Bar of the Gods ☐
   Dots Café ☐
   Cosmo Lounge ☐
   Misdemeanor Meadows ☐

Route 4 ☐
   Sextant Bar & Galley ☐
   Railside Pub ☐
   Spare Room ☐
   Korner Pocket ☐

www.ingramcontent.com/pod-product-compliance
Lightning Source LLC
Chambersburg PA
CBHW070032030426
42335CB00017B/2396